Keys to Quick Vocabulary

First Edition 2013

Copyright 2013 by Eugene Williams, Sr.

Illustrations provided by Tyrone Hardeman

ISBN   97809838952-4-4

Academic Resources Unlimited, Incorporated

P.O. Box 2122 Upper Marlboro, MD 20773

(301) 768-8316

groundedissues@gmail.com

Table of Contents

Introduction

This vocabulary book is designed to provide you with nouns, verbs, and adjectives that will improve the quality of your essays and research papers in secondary school and college. Moreover the words that you learn from this book will help you communicate more effectively in the workplace, in front of audiences, in conversations with the media, and on job interviews. Most importantly, if you are a high school student, it will help you to improve your performance on the SAT and various standardized state tests.

Unlike many vocabulary development books, it introduces new words through the use of cluster grouping and word searches. The words are grouped into clusters in order to enhance your ability to memorize their definitions. If you like to do word searches, this book will intrigue and engage you because the word searches in this book expose you to words that you may not have seen before. Secondly, you will be exposed to word charts that will include: words, their definitions, and the ways that they are used in four basic types of sentences (simple, compound, complex, and compound complex). Seeing these types of sentences will expose you to the types of writing found in textbooks, magazines, newspaper articles, columns, and editorials. These types of sentences can also serve as good models for writing assignments in high school and college English composition classes.

Make use of technology in order to enhance the effectiveness of this book. If you see words that you have difficulty pronouncing as you use this book, use the Dictionary.com application available through the app store on your smartphone. Touch the pronunciation key and listen to the words as many times as you need. Under the direction of your English teacher, use Dictionary.com when discussing these words. Compare the definitions of the word list on this book with the one listed on Dictionary.com and find out what part of speech each word is. Knowing the parts of speech also helps to improve your writing.

Note to the Students

With an extensive vocabulary you can read, write and earn high verbal scores on the SATs for admission to a four year institution and the placement test taken for admission to a community college that you plan to attend.

You need a good vocabulary with the appreciation for words to enhance your writing-paragraphs and essays. Descriptive adjectives give your writing an "umph", everlasting life.

Knowing some of the words in this book will also help you to speak with clarity and power. Your professors and supervisors on the job in the world want you to "stand and deliver" with the appropriate words. The words in this book will help you.

Note to the Life Long Learner and Career Builder

Knowing the definition of words and how to use them effectively in writing and speaking is so important and being able to pronounce them is equally as important.

This guide is designed to help you know, define, pronounce and use the words in well developed sentences.

With your technological device and a Dictionary.com application, you can not only increase your vocabulary, you can also entertain yourself. Use your device to compare the definition in the guide with those on Dictionary your device to compare the definition in the guide with those on Dictionary.com.

Introduce yourself first to the words through the word searches and charts, a unique approach to vocabulary development.

Amicus- and Greg- Cluster Word Search

```
H   R   W   T   Y   N   D   L   P   O   A   Z   U   Q   R
S   E   G   R   E   G   A   T   E   V   E   G   B   A   L
E   I   A   C   B   H   A   U   I   D   K   P   M   W   E
G   T   J   V   R   Y   G   Z   C   M   R   I   H   O   A
R   G   F   Q   D   G   G   R   E   A   T   B   I   W   T
E   X   B   A   T   E   R   N   J   Y   P   Q   Z   P   F
T   O   W   M   A   D   E   G   R   E   G   I   O   U   S
A   Y   N   I   L   C   G   A   A   I   I   P   J   E   T
G   A   P   O   A   Y   A   R   Z   M   O   B   M   D   R
E   L   L   W   B   H   T   I   V   P   I   D   L   U   A
R   Y   S   U   Q   A   E   Z   B   D   U   A   N   C   V
G   T   Q   R   E   V   J   P   Y   W   P   D   B   A   E
N   G   R   E   G   A   R   I   O   U   S   E   P   L   L
O   E   T   W   D   P   K   J   R   S   Q   F   R   F   E
C   G   U   Y   F   E   I   A   Q   T   D   H   S   V   S
```

AGGREGATE	AMIABLE	AMICABLE
AMITY	CONGREGATE	EGREGIOUS
GREGARIOUS	SEGREGATE	

The Ami- and Greg- Word Clusters

The Amicus Cluster

Word	Definition	Sentence
Amicable	Characterized by or showing friendliness.	In order to avoid fights, students must learn more **amicable** ways to settling arguments.
Amity	Peaceful relations.	A new spirit of **amity** characterizes relations between the United States and Russia now that the Cold War is over.
Amiable	Good-natured, friendly, affable	Anita's **amiable** personality made her a welcome member of our club.

The Greg Cluster

Word	Definition	Sentence
Gregarious	To like groups and the company of others.	A **gregarious** person is very outgoing and sociable.
Congregate	To flock together in a group.	During spring break, thousands of college students **congregate** at Daytona Beach.
Segregate	To keep part to separate into different groups.	Hospitals **segregate** those patients with contagious diseases into special wards.
Aggregate	To gather into a whole or mass so as to constitute the sum total.	The class treasurer announced that the **aggregate** wealth of the junior class was more than enough to pay for prom.
Egregious	To stand out from the group in a negative sense.	The home crowd complained that the referee's **egregious** call cost their team the game.

Amicus and Greg Vocabulary Practice Worksheet

Directions: To learn to spell the word, copy it in the appropriate section of this sheet. To learn or reinforce the definition, copy the definition. To effectively write sentences with each word, write a simple, compound, complex or compound complex sentence.

Word	Definition	Sentence

Matching & Sentence Completion: Amicus & Greg

MATCHING: Match the number of each word with the letter of the correct definition.

1)	Aggregate	a)	friendly
2)	Amity	b)	separate
3)	Gregarious	c)	come together
4)	Amiable	d)	good-natured
5)	Congregate	e)	liking the company of others
6)	Segregate	f)	peaceful relations
7)	Amicable	g)	sum total
8)	Egregious	h)	standing out in a negative sense

1___ 2___3___4___5___6___7___8___

SENTENCE COMPLETION: Use context clues to fill in the blanks with the correct "amicus" and "greg" words and complete the sentences correctly.

1)When the kids combined and added all of their money together, there were able to find out the amount of their_____wealth.

2)The_____college student went to many parties because he always had a need to be around large groups of people.

3)At the request of the Principal, the students were asked to _____in the auditorium , so that they could all receive their yearbooks at the same time.

4)As children, people are taught that Santa Claus is a jolly, happy, _____man who gives gifts to children for Christmas.

5)The leaders of the two warring nations signed a peace treaty in order to create a sense of _____between their countries.

Luc and Lumen, ACRI and ACER Cluster Word Search

```
D   Q   B   Z   L   P   L   O   A   C   U   M   E   N   C
T   E   A   I   U   T   U   A   T   S   R   P   W   I   E
H   Y   L   K   M   F   T   D   D   P   E   R   M   T   P
P   I   U   U   O   Q   E   G   I   I   V   A   I   Y   E
S   N   M   Q   C   A   R   H   N   B   C   D   R   P   L
U   X   I   R   P   I   A   Q   T   Z   E   U   R   E   L
O   F   N   E   V   N   D   U   Q   A   W   X   L   D   U
I   E   O   T   N   O   E   A   E   F   D   E   U   M   C
N   T   U   U   B   U   X   E   T   P   A   T   D   L   I
O   W   S   Y   A   T   I   P   G   E   C   U   V   Z   D
M   B   A   S   T   W   P   M   M   V   I   C   B   N   F
I   H   U   R   Y   M   W   J   N   K   P   A   A   W   I
R   K   E   X   A   C   E   R   B   A   T   E   C   S   H
C   V   J   Q   R   Z   Y   S   O   P   W   D   I   I   J
A   Z   R   G   P   U   B   G   X   Z   Y   E   U   Y   D
```

ACID	ACRIMONIOUS	ACUMEN
ACUTE	ELUCIDATE	EXACERBATE
LUCID	LUMINOUS	PELLUCID

Luc and Lumen, ACRI and ACER Word Clusters

The LUC and LUMEN Cluster

Word	Definition	Sentence
Lucid	Filled with light.	The dark room suddenly appeared **lucid** in the blink of an eye.
Pellucid	Crystal clear, easy to understand.	The vocabulary was very **pellucid**.
Elucidate	To bring out into the light.	Germans always try to **elucidate** the issues on the holocaust.
Luminous	Giving off light, glowing.	The sun is the most **luminous** body in the solar system.

The ACRI and ACER Cluster

Word	Definition	Sentence
Acute	Sharp; keen or very perspective.	The writer was famous for his **acute** observations about human nature.
Acumen	Refers to mental sharpness, keenness.	Her business **acumen** should be a great asset to the company.
Acid	Sharp; bitter	His **acid** criticisms of my plan were unnecessary and hurt my feelings.
Exacerbate	To make something out to be even more bitter.	His insulting comments **exacerbate** relations between the two already hostile groups.
Acrimonious	Full of spite, bitter, nasty.	Relations between the rival candidates for class president became so **acrimonious** that each refused to speak to the other.

The LUC and LUMEN, ACRI and ACER Vocabulary Practice Worksheet

Directions: To learn to spell the word, copy it in the appropriate section of this sheet. To learn or reinforce the definition, copy the definition. To effectively write sentences with each word, write a simple, compound, complex or compound complex sentence.

Word	Definition	Sentence

Matching & Sentence Completion: Luc, Lumen & Ari, Acer

MATCHING: Match the number of each word with the letter of the correct definition.

1) Acid	a) sharp; keen
2) Acute	b) sharp; bitter
3) Lucid	c) spiteful; nasty
4) Acrimonious	d) filled with light
5) Elucidate	e) glowing
6) Luminous	f) bring out into the light; clarify, make clear
7) Acumen	g) to make something more bitter or worse
8) Exacerbate	h) skill, sharpness; keenness
9) Pellucid	i) crystal clear; easy to understand

1___ 2___ 3___ 4___ 5___ 6___ 7___ 8___ 9___

SENTENCE COMPLETION: Use context clues to fill in the blanks with the correct "LUC/LUMEN" and "ACRI/ACER" words and complete the sentences correctly.

1) When Joe and Susan divorced, people called their breakup_____because, during their separation, they fought and said mean, nasty things about each other.

2) Don't _____ the situation by doing or saying things that are only going to make it worse.

3) The teacher explained concepts to his students in a straightforward, clear, and _____ way.

4) Dogs have an _____ sense of smell.

5) Her bright, white, beautiful teeth gave her a _____ smile.

Temporary, Hasty Cluster Word Search

```
E   V   B   A   T   R   A   N   S   I   E   N   T   Q   P
T   P   A   Q   E   X   B   D   Q   M   W   E   A   H   Z
W   R   H   F   F   O   W   Y   E   Y   L   V   S   R   F
B   E   J   E   P   Y   J   I   R   P   D   A   G   O   E
N   C   T   Y   M   A   Q   P   O   Q   R   N   K   J   Y
Y   I   U   J   Z   E   Y   X   L   F   H   E   Q   P   K
I   P   C   L   W   V   R   E   Z   X   P   S   O   X   S
S   I   P   E   U   A   N   A   W   N   X   C   Z   O   U
F   T   V   P   G   M   Z   V   L   U   B   D   M   V   O
Q   A   J   N   I   U   V   I   T   O   Q   N   Y   E   U
O   T   A   C   A   J   P   Y   V   A   C   T   U   C   T
D   E   S   A   C   Q   X   A   K   B   J   Z   V   H   E
R   Q   U   Y   R   A   T   N   E   M   O   M   S   K   P
J   F   M   V   Y   Z   I   O   M   Z   L   F   Z   I   M
V   T   I   M   P   U   L   S   I   V   E   W   B   N   I
```

EPHEMERAL	EVANESCENT	FLEETING
IMPETUOUS	IMPLUSIVE	MOMENTARY
PRECIPITATE	RASH	TRANSIENT

Temporary and Hasty Word Clusters

The Temporary Cluster

Word	Definition	Sentence
Momentary	For the moment. Temporary, short-lived.	There was a **momentary** pause in the audience when she fell down the stairs.
Ephemeral	Short-lived.	There are many **ephemeral** joys of childhood.
Evanescent	Quickly fading, short-lived.	She had an **evanescent** beauty in the light.
Transient	Moving from place to place.	There were many **transient** guests at the hotel.
Fleeting	Passing quickly, short-lived.	I showed a **fleeting** glance at the young man.

The Hasty Cluster

Word	Definition	Sentence
Impetuous	Lacking caution.	The young man made an **impetuous** decision on whether to go to school or not.
Rash	Acting quickly out of anger.	There was a **rash** comment made at the Black Panther meeting.
Impulsive	Acting on impulse rather than thought.	I made an **impulsive** decision to go home.
Precipitate	Hasty, lacking caution. Running "head first" into things.	The President **precipitated** an international crisis.

The Temporary and Hasty Vocabulary Practice Worksheet

Directions: To learn to spell the word, copy it in the appropriate section of this sheet. To learn or reinforce the definition, copy the definition. To effectively write sentences with each word, write a simple, compound, complex or compound complex sentence.

Word	Definition	Sentence

Matching & Sentence Completion: Temporary & Hasty

MATCHING: Match the number of each word with the letter of the correct definition.

1) Momentary
2) Ephemeral
3) Evanescent
4) Transient
5) Fleeting
6) Impetuous
7) Rash
8) Impulsive
9) Precipitate

a)temporary; moving from place to place
b)temporary; quickly fading
c) temporary; short-lived
d)temporary; for the moment
e) rushing into things "head first"
f) acting on impulse, rather than thought
g) acting quickly out of anger
h) lacking caution
i)passing quickly

1___ 2___3___4___5___6___7___8___9___

SENTENCE COMPLETION: Use context clues to fill in the blanks with the best "TEMPORARY & HASTY" cluster word choices and complete the sentences correctly.

1)Glenn acted in a_____ manner and punched John in the mouth when he said something negative about Glenn's mother.

2)Physical beauty is _____because eventually, everyone grows old.

3) Sam made an _____decision and ended up marrying a woman who was prone to engage in dangerous behavior.

4)A _____person never stays at one particular residence for very long.

5) The baseball player acted in a _____ manner by sliding "head first" into home plate without realizing that the ball had been hit over the right field wall.

Bene- or Ben and Mal Cluster

Bene- or Ben and Mal Cluster Word Search

```
S  C  G  Z  T  N  E  L  O  V  E  N  E  B  L
D  T  M  A  L  I  N  G  E  R  E  R  S  E  I
Y  G  A  W  H  P  O  L  B  M  Q  M  H  N  G
H  O  L  A  A  T  R  A  E  A  U  A  E  E  N
T  B  E  N  I  G  N  U  N  B  N  L  R  F  Q
P  Z  V  T  D  J  L  S  E  O  D  I  V  A  Z
L  X  O  E  Y  T  E  R  I  D  J  C  L  C  D
M  A  L  I  G  N  Y  T  R  E  V  I  O  T  T
A  U  E  R  S  M  C  M  W  S  X  O  C  O  V
Q  P  N  O  Y  I  J  A  A  T  D  U  K  R  O
R  F  T  Y  D  Q  M  L  B  R  J  S  M  S  L
N  E  Y  E  F  B  E  N  E  F  I  T  R  O  E
V  M  N  H  I  T  R  V  D  U  Z  B  W  P  N
Y  E  B  M  G  H  M  A  L  I  G  N  A  N  T
B  N  M  A  L  E  D  I  C  T  I  O  N  Q  A
```

BENEDICTION	BENEFACTOR	BENEFIT
BENEVOLENT	BENIGN	MALEDICTION
MALEVOLENT	MALICIOUS	MALIGN
MALIGNANT	MALINGERER	

Bene or Ben and Mal Word Clusters

The Bene/Ben Cluster

Word	Definition	Sentence
Benefit	Anything that promotes or enhances well-being.	The **benefits** of the job include two weeks of paid vacation, free use of the company fitness center and inexpensive health care.
Benevolent	Kindly, full of good will.	Contributing presents to needy children is a **benevolent** act.
Benefactor	One who does good by giving financial or other aid.	The school's new computer lab was the gift of a generous **benefactor**.
Benediction	The act of saying a blessing.	The minister gave a **benediction** at the end of the funeral service.
Benign	Kind, gentle.	The **benign** grandparents gave everything they could to their grandchildren.

The Mal Cluster

Word	Definition	Sentence
Malign	To speak badly of, to slander, defame.	Many people complained the politicians were more interesting in **maligning** each other than the issues.
Malicious	Filled with malice or ill will.	He was the unfortunate victim of a **malicious** rumor spread by a jealous rival.
Malevolent	Wishing harm to others.	Her **malevolent** remark hurt his feelings.
Malediction	Act of saying evil or a curse.	The evil wizard uttered a **malediction** against his enemies.
Malignant	Deadly, very harmful.	The **malignant** rumors severely damaged his reputation.
Malingerer	Someone who procrastinates or avoids work.	Danielle turned out to be a **malingerer** who rarely did her chores.

The Bene/Ben and Mal Vocabulary Practice Worksheet

Directions: To learn to spell the word, copy it in the appropriate section of this sheet. To learn or reinforce the definition, copy the definition. To effectively write sentences with each word, write a simple, compound, complex or compound complex sentence.

Word	Definition	Sentence

Matching & Sentence Completion: Bene/Ben & Mal

MATCHING: Match the number of each word with the letter of the correct definition.

1) Benefit	a) one who gives financial aid
2) Benevolent	b) speak badly of; slander; defame
3) Benefactor	c) procrastinator; one who avoids work
4) Benediction	d) a curse
5) Malign	e) deadly;harmful
6) Malicious	f) anything that promotes or enhances well-being
7) Malevolent	g) kindly; full of good will
8) Malediction	h) a blessing
9) Malignant	i) filled with malice or ill will
10) Malingerer	j) wishing harm to others

1___ 2___3___4___5___6___7___8___9___10___

SENTENCE COMPLETION: Use context clues to fill in the blanks with the correct "BEN/BENE" and "MAL" words in order to complete the sentences correctly.

1)At the beginning of any church service, or before a meal is served at a religious event , a pastor will usually give a _____ in order to bless the congregation, or the food.

2)A student who is a _____usually waits until the "last minute" to complete homework and do school projects.

3)Parents are natural _____(s) because they provide their children with food, clothing and money.

4)A_____ tumor can cause death, but benign tumors do not.

5)Most children consider Santa Claus to be_____because he's jolly, promotes good will, and gives presents to kids.

Secret and Stubborn Cluster

Secret and Stubborn Cluster Word Search

```
H   Z   U   C   E   N   I   T   S   E   D   N   A   L   C
A   W   S   O   R   C   B   S   R   E   Z   Q   X   I   Z
L   S   R   V   T   L   R   G   Y   D   P   R   V   N   X
E   N   U   E   B   A   D   E   G   G   O   D   B   T   T
J   T   J   R   N   N   Q   L   I   T   X   U   M   R   O
O   P   A   T   E   D   X   E   K   K   W   Y   J   A   B
F   H   G   Q   A   P   J   N   H   A   F   H   O   N   S
U   K   R   Z   D   G   T   O   F   D   S   T   U   S   T
R   U   T   B   W   E   L   I   S   O   C   L   T   I   I
T   Q   R   C   Y   N   O   G   T   D   B   A   W   G   N
I   X   U   Y   O   T   Z   E   A   O   U   E   H   E   A
V   H   B   J   H   Q   G   D   V   G   U   L   G   N   T
E   O   B   D   U   R   A   T   E   R   D   S   M   T   E
E   T   D   K   F   V   N   W   T   B   H   V   L   N   R
L   R   E   C   A   L   C   I   T   R   A   N   T   Y   F
```

CLANDESTINE	COVERT	DOGGED
FURTIVE	INTRANSIGENT	OBSURATE
OBSTINATE	RECALCITRANT	STEALTHY
SURREPTITIOUSLY		

Secret and Stubborn Word Clusters

The Stubborn Cluster

Word	Definition	Sentence
Obstinate	Stubborn and unyielding	The **obstinate** growth of the weeds made it hard to obtain.
Obdurate	Stubborn and unyielding, particularly hardhearted and callous.	There was an **obdurate** sinner in my presence.
Intransigent	Stubborn and unyielding, uncompromising.	The defendant's lawyer was very **intransigent** when offered a settlement deal.
Recalcitrant	Stubborn and unyielding, particularly to authority.	The kids in the daycare were very **recalcitrant** to their caretaker.
Dogged	Stubborn and unyielding, not easily subdued.	The **dogged** worked was not energetic at work at all.

The Secret Cluster

Word	Definition	Sentence
Clandestine	Characterized by, done in or executed with secrecy or concealment.	Their **clandestine** meetings went undiscovered for two years.
Surreptitiously	Obtained, done, made, etc., by stealth; secret or unauthorized.	He was watching her **surreptitiously** as she waited in the hotel lobby.
Stealthy	Done, characterized by or acting in secret.	The tiger **stealthy** while stalking his prey.
Covert	Concealed; secret; disguised.	The government gave **covert** funding to the military operations.
Furtive	Taken, done, used, etc., by secret	She approached me in a **furtive** manner.

The Secret & Stubborn Vocabulary Practice Worksheet

Directions: To learn to spell the word, copy it in the appropriate section of this sheet. To learn or reinforce the definition, copy the definition. To effectively write sentences with each word, write a simple, compound, complex or compound complex sentence.

Word	Definition	Sentence

Matching & Sentence Completion: Secret & Stubborn

MATCHING: Match the number of each word with the letter of the correct definition.

1) Obstinate	a)Taken , done, or used by secret
2) Obdurate	b)concealed; secret; disguised
3) Intransigent	c) done or acting in secret
4) Recalcitrant	d) done secretly; unauthorized
5) Dogged	e) done secretly with a concealed purpose
6) Clandestine	f) not easily subdued
7) Surreptitiously	g) unyielding to authority
8) Stealthy	h) uncompromising
9) Covert	i) unyielding
10) Furtive	j)particularly hardhearted, callous

1___ 2___3___4___5___6___7___8___9___10____

SENTENCE COMPLETION: Use context clues to fill in the blanks with the best "SECRET"& "STUBBORN" cluster word choices and complete the sentences correctly.

1)Whenever Mike gets in an argument, he engages in _____behavior, because he refuses to even attempt to compromise, or see things from another person's point of view.

2)Spies often have to use disguises to conceal their true identities when they work on _____operations.

3)The _____child was known for disobeying parents, teachers, and other authority figures.

4)Romeo and Juliet had to have_____meetings because they didn't want their parents to know that they were lovers.

5)The _____villain of the story used whatever tactics that were needed to achieve his goals, and wouldn't change his tactics regardless of who they hurt.

Plac and Chron Cluster

Plac and Chron Cluster Word Search

```
Q   K   L   Y   P   W   R   U   P   S   F   H   L   C   N
F   S   Y   P   L   A   G   Y   E   X   N   O   H   O   X
Y   Y   P   L   A   C   A   T   E   Q   B   R   I   M   Q
K   N   E   A   C   G   T   Z   W   M   O   H   U   P   L
M   C   G   W   I   V   Y   A   I   N   G   A   E   L   F
V   H   B   I   G   P   R   B   I   J   C   H   W   A   E
P   R   A   M   O   D   Q   C   K   Z   O   D   S   C   L
L   O   Q   V   L   Z   P   H   T   Q   B   M   P   E   B
A   N   D   Z   O   V   E   J   P   L   A   C   V   N   A
C   I   V   A   N   C   N   B   F   E   Y   J   F   T   C
I   Z   U   G   O   C   H   R   O   N   I   C   L   E   A
D   E   P   U   R   G   K   O   P   G   D   A   E   G   L
T   H   Z   J   H   Z   V   H   U   Q   F   H   U   K   P
Z   A   N   A   C   H   R   O   N   I   S   M   G   B   M
P   Q   B   F   R   X   G   U   M   F   A   Y   K   P   I
```

ANACHRONISM   CHRONIC   CHRONICLE

CHRONOLOGICAL   COMPLACENT   IMPLACABLE

PLACATE   PLACID   SYNCHRONIZE

Plac and Chron Cluster Word Charts

The Plac Cluster

Word	Definition	Sentence
Placid	To be outwardly calm and composed.	The coach's **placid** disposition enabled her to remain calm and focused despite the raucous crowd.
Placate	To appease or pacify.	The babysitter **placated** the crying baby by allowing him to eat his favorite candy.
Complacent	Pleased, especially with oneself or one's merits, advantages, etc.	After receiving a huge signing bonus, the rookie became **complacent** and soon lost his starting position.
Implacable	Incapable of appeasement and therefore relentless.	The presence of two such **implacable** foes made it impossible to negotiate a peace treaty.

The Chron Cluster

Word	Definition	Sentence
Chronological	Arranged in order of occurrence	After completing her first draft, the novelist decided to tell her story in **chronological** order, rather than shifting from present to past.
Synchronize	To occur together at the same time simultaneous.	We **synchronized** our clocks so we can arrive at the prom at precisely the same time.
Chronicle	A record of events in order of time.	His **chronicle** of the Civil War began with the firing of Fort Sumter and ended with Lee's surrender at Appomatox.
Chronic	Refers to a habit, condition, or disease that continues over a long period of time.	Diane was a **chronic** complainer who annoyed everyone in the department.
Anachronism	Refers to something that is not happening in its proper time.	The clock that strikes twelve in Shakespeare's Julius Caesar is an **anachronism** since there were no striking clocks in ancient Rome.

The Plac and Chron Vocabulary Practice Worksheet

Directions: To learn to spell the word, copy it in the appropriate section of this sheet. To learn or reinforce the definition, copy the definition. To effectively write sentences with each word, write a simple, compound, complex or compound complex sentence.

Word	Definition	Sentence

Matching & Sentence Completion: Plac & Chron

MATCHING: Match the number of each word with the letter of the correct definition.

1) Chronological   a) incapable of appeasement; cannot be pleased
2) Synchronize   b) to appease, please, or pacify
3) Chronicle   c) pleased with oneself
4) Chronic   d) arranged in order of occurrence
5) Anachronism   e) calm, composed, peaceful
6) Placid   f) to make things occur at the same time
7) Placate   g) refers to habit, condition or disease that occurs over time
8) Complacent   h) something that is not happening in its proper time
9) Implacable   i) a record of events in order of time that they occurred

1___ 2___ 3___ 4___ 5___ 6___ 7___ 8___ 9___

SENTENCE COMPLETION: Use context clues to fill in the blanks with the correct "PLAC " and "CHRON" words in order to complete the sentences correctly.

1)Since newspapers are a record of events in the order that they occurred, the names of several newspapers have the word "_____" in them.

2)No matter how many times we fed, held, or sang to him, the _____baby would not stop crying.

3)If you lived in the 1700's and saw someone with a cell phone, that would be an example of an _____.

4)A _____person is so satisfied and content with his current situation that he feels no desire or need to improve it.

5)Let's _____our clocks so that our alarms will go off at exactly the same time.

IN, IM, UN, AB Cluster Word Search

```
I   M   P   I   O   L   S   X   W   K   G   V   Y   E   A
W   G   U   N   O   R   T   H   O   D   O   X   B   L   B
T   I   N   C   O   R   R   I   G   I   B   L   E   B   E
E   N   F   O   Y   E   Q   N   U   N   S   U   T   A   R
D   V   E   R   J   L   Z   T   N   T   C   N   A   P   R
G   I   T   P   K   B   V   E   C   E   A   S   R   P   A
J   O   T   O   L   A   F   R   O   D   T   C   D   A   N
E   L   E   R   Q   P   Y   M   R   E   H   A   I   L   T
T   A   R   E   D   P   M   I   G   D   D   T   S   F   R
A   B   E   A   F   A   G   N   H   N   E   H   D   N   E
C   L   D   L   B   L   D   A   I   U   Q   E   F   U   R
I   E   L   M   J   F   A   B   K   O   F   D   H   O   I
D   S   D   Z   I   N   G   L   M   F   Z   A   H   D   D
B   N   U   I   D   U   H   E   G   N   X   B   F   I   B
A   D   I   P   E   R   T   N   I   U   A   D   V   J   A
```

ABDICATE
ABSTAIN
INCORRIGIBLE
INVIOLABLE
UNFOUNDED

ABERRANT
IMPIOUS
INTERMINABLE
UNFETTERED
UNORTHODOX

ABHOR
INCORPOREAL
INTREPID
UNFLAPPABLE
UNSCATHED

IN, IM, UN, AB Cluster Word Charts

The IN and IM Cluster

Word	Definition	Sentence
Interminable	To end.	The trail was supposed to be short, but the prosecutor's **interminable** questions dragged out the trail for days.
Incorrigible	Cannot be corrected or reformed.	The **incorrigible** youth was finally expelled from school.
Impious	Lacking reverence; disrespectful.	His loud talking and other **impious** behavior offended many worshippers.
Incorporeal	Having no body or substance.	Many people believe that **incorporeal** beings exist and can influence human behavior.
Intrepid	Brave and courageous.	The general praised the **intrepid** men and women who volunteered to take part in the dangerous mission.
Inviolable	Secure and cannot be violated.	The U.N. Security Council guaranteed that the new countries' boundaries would be protected and therefore **inviolable**.

The UN and AB Cluster

Word	Definition	Sentence
Abdicate	To give up or renounce.	Mary Queen of Scots was forced to **abdicate** her throne in 1567.
Aberrant	Departing from the right, normal or usual course.	Modern day cancer focuses on cutting off nutrition to **aberrant** cells.
Abhor	Regard with extreme aversion, loathe or detest.	While he absolutely **abhorred** his opponents' views, they had the right to express them.
Abstain	To hold oneself back voluntarily.	They both promised to **abstain** from eating meat after watching the documentary.
Unfettered	To free from restraint; liberate.	Their aim was to give the journalist **unfettered** access to the company's records.
Unflappable	Not easily upset or confused.	Helen was **unflappable** when she was questioned by the lawyer.
Unfounded	Not based on fact, realistic considerations.	The candidate said the charges against him were completely **unfounded**.
Unorthodox	Contrary to what is usual, traditional or accepted.	His **unorthodox** studying methods helped him to pass the final.
Unscathed	Unharmed; uninjured.	She walked away from the accident **unscathed**.

The IN and IM Vocabulary Practice Worksheet

Directions: To learn to spell the word, copy it in the appropriate section of this sheet. To learn or reinforce the definition, copy the definition. To effectively write sentences with each word, write a simple, compound, complex or compound complex sentence.

Word	Definition	Sentence

The UN and AB Vocabulary Practice Worksheet

Directions: To learn to spell the word, copy it in the appropriate section of this sheet. To learn or reinforce the definition, copy the definition. To effectively write sentences with each word, write a simple, compound, complex or compound complex sentence.

Word	Definition	Sentence

Matching & Sentence Completion: IN, IM, UN, AB

MATCHING: Match the number of each word with the letter of the correct definition.

1) interminable	a) unharmed; uninjured
2) incorrigible	b) contrary to what is usual, traditional, or accepted
3) impious	c) not factual or realistic
4) incorporeal	d) not easily upset or confused
5) intrepid	e) free from restraint; liberated
6) inviolable	f) to hold oneself back voluntarily
7) abdicate	g) to hate, loathe, or detest
8) aberrant	h) departing from the right, normal, or usual course
9) abhor	i) to give up or renounce
10) abstain	j) secure and cannot be violated
11) unfettered	k) brave and courageous; without fear
12) unflappable	l) having no body or substance
13) unfounded	m) lacking reverence; disrespectful
14) unorthodox	n) cannot be corrected or reformed
15) unscathed	o) to no end; neverending

1___ 2___ 3___ 4___ 5___ 6___ 7___ 8___ 9___ 10___ 11___ 12___ 13___ 14___ 15___

SENTENCE COMPLETION: Use context clues to fill in the blanks with the correct "IN, IM, AB, & UN" cluster words in order to complete the sentences correctly.

1) A student who keeps engaging in negative behavior over and over again, no matter how many times the teacher tries to correct them, will most likely have to go to the Principal's office for _____ behavior.

2) Being loud and unruly during silent prayer in church will cause people to view you as being_____.

3) When someone tells you that they absolutely dislike you and everything you stand for, then they probably _____ you.

4)When the slave received his freedom, and the chains and shackles were removed from his wrists and ankles, he felt _____.

5)The king was prepared to _____ his throne and become a poor , common man if that's what he would have to do in order to marry the woman he truly loved.

Recall and Repeat Cluster Word Search

```
Q   U   G   B   M   P   J   H   Z   C   G   E   V   S   R
A   R   E   R   V   I   Z   V   T   G   S   E   F   E   N
M   E   B   W   E   Q   T   K   S   D   W   Q   D   B   R
G   N   E   D   X   V   D   O   U   U   H   U   D   O   E
B   O   F   H   G   I   I   R   R   N   N   T   A   O   V
S   V   H   L   D   Y   H   T   G   D   P   O   L   S   Y
D   A   S   O   S   F   J   S   A   S   H   R   R   F   G
H   T   D   I   U   D   G   N   D   L   D   C   H   H   R
R   E   G   K   M   S   T   F   X   H   I   H   D   P   E
E   Q   H   G   L   C   D   B   H   U   T   Z   U   Z   V
F   Y   S   D   H   V   J   D   I   T   S   W   E   V   O
H   K   F   A   D   D   G   U   E   W   G   O   B   P   K
W   H   K   C   R   E   S   U   R   G   E   O   Q   B   E
F   T   O   H   D   J   F   S   A   T   J   S   S   N   S
H   R   E   M   U   N   E   R   A   T   I   O   N   L   C
```

REDUNDANT   RENOVATE   RESURGE
REVITALIZE   REVOKE   REMUNERATION

Recall and Repeat Cluster Word Charts

The IN and IM Cluster

Word	Definition	Sentence
Revoke	To recall or cancel.	His driver's license was **revoked**.
Revitalize	To restore the vitality or life of, to revive.	Everyone thought the surfer drowned but the paramedics **revitalized** him.
Renovate	To make new again.	The new owners **renovated** the stadium by adding a high-tech scoreboard and more comfortable seats.
Resurge	To rise again or surge again.	The interest in 1960s music is currently **resurging**.
Redundant	Excessively repetitious.	The student's essay was filled with **redundant** phrases.
Remuneration	To give back.	He received little **remuneration** for his services.

The Recall and Repeat Vocabulary Practice Worksheet

Directions: To learn to spell the word, copy it in the appropriate section of this sheet. To learn or reinforce the definition, copy the definition. To effectively write sentences with each word, write a simple, compound, complex or compound complex sentence.

Word	Definition	Sentence

Matching & Sentence Completion: Recall & Repeat

MATCHING: Match the number of each word with the letter of the correct definition.

1) revoke   a)to give back or pay back
2) revitalize   b) to rise again
3) renovate   c) excessively repetitious
4) resurge   d)to give life; to restore life; revive
5) redundant   e)to recall or cancel
6) remuneration   f) to make new again

1___ 2___3___4___5___6___

SENTENCE COMPLETION: Use context clues to fill in the blanks with the correct "RECALL" and "REPEAT" cluster words in order to complete the sentences correctly.

1) I loaned you $20 back when you were unemployed. Now that you have a job, I expect to receive _____.

2)The house was old and deserted so I decided to _____it and sell it as if it were brand new.

3)When you say the same thing over and over again, people accuse you of being_____.

4)He had so many tickets for speeding and "driving under the influence" that the judge ruled to _____his driver's license.

5)He was tired and out of shape so he ate healthy and exercised in order to _____his body.

Solutions to Word Searches

Amicus- and Greg-

H	R	W	T	Y	N	D	L	P	O	A	Z	U	Q	R
S	**E**	**G**	**R**	**E**	**G**	**A**	T	**E**	V	E	G	B	**A**	L
E	I	A	C	B	H	**A**	U	I	D	K	P	**M**	W	E
G	T	J	V	R	Y	**G**	Z	C	M	R	**I**	H	O	A
R	G	F	Q	D	G	**G**	R	E	A	**T**	B	I	W	T
E	X	B	A	T	E	**R**	N	J	**Y**	P	Q	Z	P	F
T	O	W	M	A	D	**E**	**G**	**R**	**E**	**G**	**I**	**O**	**U**	**S**
A	Y	N	I	L	C	**G**	A	**A**	I	I	P	J	E	T
G	A	P	O	A	Y	**A**	R	Z	**M**	O	B	M	D	R
E	L	L	W	B	H	**T**	I	V	P	**I**	D	L	U	A
R	Y	S	U	Q	A	**E**	Z	B	D	U	**A**	N	C	V
G	T	Q	R	E	V	J	P	Y	W	P	D	**B**	A	E
N	**G**	**R**	**E**	**G**	**A**	**R**	**I**	**O**	**U**	**S**	E	P	**L**	L
O	E	T	W	D	P	K	J	R	S	Q	F	R	F	**E**
C	G	U	Y	F	E	I	A	Q	T	D	H	S	V	S

Luc and Lumen, ACRI and ACER

D	Q	B	Z	L	P	L	O	**A**	**C**	**U**	**M**	**E**	**N**	C
T	**E**	A	I	U	T	U	A	T	S	R	P	W	I	E
H	Y	**L**	K	M	F	T	D	**D**	P	E	R	M	T	**P**
P	I	**U**	**U**	O	Q	E	G	I	**I**	V	A	I	Y	**E**
S	N	**M**	Q	**C**	A	R	H	N	B	**C**	D	R	P	**L**
U	X	**I**	R	P	**I**	A	Q	T	Z	E	**U**	R	E	**L**
O	F	**N**	E	V	N	**D**	U	Q	A	W	X	**L**	D	**U**
I	E	**O**	T	N	O	E	**A**	E	F	D	**E**	U	M	**C**
N	T	**U**	U	B	U	X	E	**T**	P	A	**T**	D	L	**I**
O	W	**S**	Y	A	T	I	P	G	**E**	C	**U**	V	Z	**D**
M	B	A	S	T	W	P	M	M	V	I	**C**	B	N	F
I	H	U	R	Y	M	W	J	N	K	P	**A**	A	W	I
R	K	**E**	**X**	**A**	**C**	**E**	**R**	**B**	**A**	**T**	**E**	**C**	S	H
C	V	J	Q	R	Z	Y	S	O	P	W	D	I	**I**	J
A	Z	R	G	P	U	B	G	X	Z	Y	E	U	Y	**D**

73

Temporary, Hasty

E	V	B	A	T	R	A	N	S	I	E	N	T	Q	P
T	P	A	Q	E	X	B	D	Q	M	W	E	A	H	Z
W	R	H	F	F	O	W	Y	E	Y	L	V	S	R	F
B	E	J	E	P	Y	J	I	R	P	D	A	G	O	E
N	C	T	Y	M	A	Q	P	O	Q	R	N	K	J	Y
Y	I	U	J	Z	E	Y	X	L	F	H	E	Q	P	K
I	P	C	L	W	V	R	E	Z	X	P	S	O	X	S
S	I	P	E	U	A	N	A	W	N	X	C	Z	O	U
F	T	V	P	G	M	Z	V	L	U	B	E	M	V	O
Q	A	J	N	I	U	V	I	T	O	Q	N	Y	E	U
O	T	A	C	A	J	P	Y	V	A	C	T	U	C	T
D	E	S	A	C	Q	X	A	K	B	J	Z	V	H	E
R	Q	U	Y	R	A	T	N	E	M	O	M	S	K	P
J	F	M	V	Y	Z	I	O	M	Z	L	F	Z	I	M
V	T	I	M	P	U	L	S	I	V	E	W	B	N	I

Bene- or Ben and Mal

S	C	G	Z	T	N	E	L	O	V	E	N	E	B	L
D	T	M	A	L	I	N	G	E	R	E	R	S	E	I
Y	G	A	W	H	P	O	L	B	M	Q	M	H	N	G
H	O	L	A	A	T	R	A	E	A	U	A	E	E	N
T	B	E	N	I	G	N	U	N	B	N	L	R	F	Q
P	Z	V	T	D	J	L	S	E	O	D	I	V	A	Z
L	X	O	E	Y	T	E	R	I	D	J	C	L	C	D
M	A	L	I	G	N	Y	T	R	E	V	I	O	T	T
A	U	E	R	S	M	C	M	W	S	X	O	C	O	V
Q	P	N	O	Y	I	J	A	A	T	D	U	K	R	O
R	F	T	Y	D	Q	M	L	B	R	J	S	M	S	L
N	E	Y	E	F	B	E	N	E	F	I	T	R	O	E
V	M	N	H	I	T	R	V	D	U	Z	B	W	P	N
Y	E	B	M	G	H	M	A	L	I	G	N	A	N	T
B	N	M	A	L	E	D	I	C	T	I	O	N	Q	A

Secret and Stubborn

```
H  Z  U  C  E  N  I  T  S  E  D  N  A  L  C
A  W  S  O  R  C  B  S  R  E  Z  Q  X  I  Z
L  S  R  V  T  L  R  G  Y  D  P  R  V  N  X
E  N  U  E  B  A  D  E  G  G  O  D  B  T  T
J  T  J  R  N  N  Q  L  I  T  X  U  M  R  O
O  P  A  T  E  D  X  E  K  K  W  Y  J  A  B
F  H  G  Q  A  P  J  N  H  A  F  H  O  N  S
U  K  R  Z  D  G  T  O  F  D  S  T  U  S  T
R  U  T  B  W  E  L  I  S  O  C  L  T  I  I
T  Q  R  C  Y  N  O  G  T  D  B  A  W  G  N
I  X  U  Y  O  T  Z  E  A  O  U  E  H  E  A
V  H  B  J  H  Q  G  D  V  G  U  L  G  N  T
E  O  B  S  U  R  A  T  E  R  D  S  M  T  E
E  T  D  K  F  V  N  W  T  B  H  V  L  N  R
L  R  E  C  A  L  C  I  T  R  A  N  T  Y  F
```

Plac and Chron

```
Q  K  L  Y  P  W  R  U  P  S  F  H  L  C  N
F  S  Y  P  L  A  G  Y  E  X  N  O  H  O  X
Y  Y  P  L  A  C  A  T  E  Q  B  R  I  M  Q
K  N  E  A  C  G  T  Z  W  M  O  H  U  P  L
M  C  G  W  I  V  Y  A  I  N  G  A  E  L  F
V  H  B  I  G  P  R  B  I  J  C  H  W  A  E
P  R  A  M  O  D  Q  C  K  Z  O  D  S  C  L
L  O  Q  V  L  Z  P  H  T  Q  B  M  P  E  B
A  N  D  Z  O  V  E  J  P  L  A  C  V  N  A
C  I  V  A  N  C  N  B  F  E  Y  J  F  T  C
I  Z  U  G  O  C  H  R  O  N  I  C  L  E  A
D  E  P  U  R  G  K  O  P  G  D  A  E  G  L
T  H  Z  J  H  Z  V  H  U  Q  F  H  U  K  P
Z  A  N  A  C  H  R  O  N  I  S  M  G  B  M
P  Q  B  F  R  X  G  U  M  F  A  Y  K  P  I
```

IN, IM, UN, AB

```
I  M  P  I  O  U  S  X  W  K  G  V  Y  E  A
W  G  U  N  O  R  T  H  O  D  O  X  B  L  B
T  I  N  C  O  R  R  I  G  I  B  L  E  B  E
E  N  F  O  Y  E  Q  N  U  N  S  U  T  A  R
D  V  E  R  J  L  Z  T  N  T  C  N  A  P  R
G  I  T  P  K  B  V  E  C  E  A  S  R  P  A
J  O  T  O  L  A  F  R  O  D  T  C  D  A  N
E  L  E  R  Q  P  Y  M  R  E  H  A  I  L  T
T  A  R  E  D  P  M  I  G  D  D  T  S  F  R
A  B  E  A  F  A  G  N  N  E  H  D  N  E
C  L  D  L  B  L  D  A  I  U  Q  E  F  U  R
I  E  L  M  J  F  A  B  K  O  F  D  H  O  I
D  S  D  Z  I  N  G  L  M  F  Z  A  H  D  D
B  N  U  I  D  U  H  E  G  N  X  B  F  I  B
A  D  I  P  E  R  T  N  I  U  A  D  V  J  A
```

Recall and Repeat

```
Q  U  G  B  M  P  J  H  Z  C  G  E  V  S  R
A  R  E  R  V  I  Z  V  T  G  S  E  F  E  N
M  E  B  W  E  Q  T  K  S  D  W  Q  D  B  R
G  N  E  D  X  V  D  O  U  U  H  U  D  O  E
B  O  F  H  G  I  I  R  R  N  N  T  A  O  V
S  V  H  L  D  Y  H  T  G  D  P  O  L  S  Y
D  A  S  O  S  F  J  S  A  S  H  R  R  F  G
H  T  D  I  U  D  G  N  D  L  D  C  H  H  R
R  E  G  K  M  S  T  F  X  H  I  H  D  P  E
E  Q  H  G  L  C  D  B  H  U  T  Z  U  Z  V
F  Y  S  D  H  V  J  D  I  T  S  W  E  V  O
H  K  F  A  D  D  G  U  E  W  G  O  B  P  K
W  H  K  C  R  E  S  U  R  G  E  O  Q  B  E
F  T  O  H  D  J  F  S  A  T  J  S  S  N  S
H  R  E  M  U  N  E  R  A  T  I  O  N  L  C
```

Answer Key to Matching & Sentence Completion

ANSWERS TO "AMICUS" & "GREG" Words

Matching: 1) G   2) F   3) E   4) D   5) C   6) B   7) A   8) H

Sentence Completion: 1) Aggregate 2) Gregarious 3) Congregation 4) Amiable 5) Amity

ANSWERS TO "LUC/LUMEN" & "ACRI/ACER" Words

Matching: 1) B   2) A   3) D   4) C   5) F   6) E   7) H   8) G   9) I

Sentence Completion: 1) Acrimonious 2) Exacerbate 3) Pellucid   4) Acute   5) Luminous

ANSWERS TO TEMPORARY & HASTY CLUSTER Words

Matching: 1) D   2) C   3) B   4) A   5) I   6) H   7) G   8) F   9) E

Sentence Completion: 1) Rash 2) Evanescent 3) Impetuous 4) Transient 5) Precipitate

ANSWERS TO "BENE/BEN" & "MAL" Words

Matching: 1) F   2) G   3) A   4) H   5) B   6) I   7) J   8) D   9) E   10) C

Sentence Completion: 1) Benediction 2) Malingerer 3) Benefactors 4) Malignant 5) Benevolent

ANSWERS TO SECRET & STUBBORN CLUSTER Words

Matching: 1) I   2) J   3) H   4) G   5) F   6) E   7) D   8) C   9) B   10) A

Sentence Completion: 1) Intransigent 2) Covert 3) Recalcitrant 4) Clandestine 5) Obdurate

ANSWERS TO "PLAC" & "CHRON" Words

Matching: 1) D   2) F   3) I   4) G   5) H   6) E   7) B   8) C   9) A

Sentence Completion: 1) Chronicle   2) Implacable   3) Anachronism   4) Complacent
5) Synchronize

ANSWERS TO "IN, IM, AB, & UN" Words

Matching: 1) O   2) N   3) M   4) L   5) K   6) J   7) I   8) H   9) G   10) F   11) E
12) D   13) C   14) B   15) A

Sentence Completion: 1) Incorrigible   2) Impious   3) Abhor   4) Unfettered   5) Abdicate

ANSWERS TO RECALL & REPEAT CLUSTER Words

Matching: 1) E   2) D   3) F   4) B   5) C   6) A

Sentence Completion: 1) Remuneration   2) Renovate   3) Redundant   4) Revoke   5) Revitalize

Glossary of Words to Know

Adjectives and Verbs

A

Abashed *adj.* Embarrassed or ashamed.

Aloof *adj.* Distant; remote; standoffish.

Ascend *v.* To rise; climb.

Authoritarian *adj.* Expecting or demanding absolute obedience.

Abiding *adj.* Lasting or enduring.

Amicable *adj.* Having or showing a friendly attitude.

Ascetic *adj.* Severe; stern.

Avenge *v.* To take revenge on behalf of.

Accost *v.* To approach and speak to in an aggressive or hostile manner.

Ardent *adj.* Displaying great warmth of feeling; passionate.

Auspicious *adj.* Promising success; favorable.

Averse *adj.* Unwilling; deeply reluctant

B

Balmy *adj.* Soothingly fragrant; mild and pleasant.

Beseech *v.* To beg eagerly.

Bolster *v.* To support; reinforce.

Beguiling *v.* Charming; pleasing.

Biased *adj.* Marked by an unfair preference; prejudiced.

Boisterous *adj.* Loud, noisy and unrestrained.

Bereft *adj.* Suffering the death of a loved one; deprived of someone or something important.

Blatant *adj.* Completely obvious

Brooding *adj.* Having a moody or depressed disposition.

C

Cajole *v.* To persuade by pleasant words, flattery, or false promises.

Cavort *v.* To leap or romp about.

Commandeer *v.* To take control of by force.

Coveted *adj.* Greedily wished for.

Calibrated *adj.* Marked with measurements.

Censure *v.* To criticize severely, to blame.

Commiserate *v.* To express sorrow or pity for another's trouble.

Convey *v.* To make known; communicate.

Careen *v.* To rush carelessly

Churlish *adj.* Rude or ill-tempered.

Construe *v.* To interpret.

Cultivate *v.* To seek to become familiar with.

D

Decipher *v.* To read for interpret something unclear; to figure out.
Defiant *adj.* Boldly resistant of an opposing force or authority.
Dexterous *adj.* Skillful; clever.

Dissenting *adj.* Disagreeing; having a different opinion.

Decorous *adj.* Behaving in a manner appropriate to the occasion; proper.
Despondent *adj.* Without hope; dejected.

Dispel *v.* To scatter; drive away.
Dithering *adj.* Acting in a nervous or uncertain way.

Default *v.* To fail to keep a promise, especially a promise to repay a loan.
Destined *adj.* Determined beforehand.

Disperse *v.* To scatter.

Droll *adj.* Amusingly odd or comical.

E

Eloquent *adj.* Vividly expressive

Embroider *v.* To add imaginative details to; ornament.
Ethereal *adj.* Not earthly; heavenly
Exasperated *adj.* Made impatient or angry; annoyed.

Embody *v.* To give concrete shape to; personify or represent.
Enticing *adj.* Luring; tempting.

Evoke *v.* To call to mind.

Exhilarate *v.* To make merry or lively.

Encumber *v.* To burden.

Entreat *v.* To ask earnestly.

Exalt *v.* To glorify, praise, or honor.
Exorbitant *adj.* Much too high; excessive.

F

Fallible *adj.* Capable to being wrong or mistaken.

Feigned *adj.* Not real; pretended.
Formidable *adj.* Inspiring admiration, awe or fear.

Fanatical *adj.* Extremely enthusiastic.

Fetter *v.* To restrain with chains or shackles.
Fulfill *v.* To achieve; make a reality.

Fathom *v.* To penetrate the meaning or understand the nature of.
Flail *v.* To move vigorously or erratically.
Futile *adj.* Having no useful result; without effect.

G

Garish *adj.* Too bright or gaudy.

Goad *v.* To urge

Grotesque *adj.* Odd, twisted, or bizarre.

H

Haggard *adj.* Appearing worn and exhausted.

Harass *v.* To persistently brother or torment.

Haughty *adj.* Proud; arrogant.

Hedge *v.* To avoid giving a direct answer.

Heedless *adj.* Unmindful; careless.

Hoist *v.* To raise or haul up.

Hone *v.* To sharpen.

Hospitable *adj.* Welcoming; cordial.

Hypothermic *adj.* Having an abnormally low body temperature.

I

Imminent *adj.* About to occur.

Imperative *adj.* Absolutely necessary.

Inaugurate *v.* To make a formal beginning of.

Incredulous *adj.* Doubtful; disbelieving.

Indolent *adj.* Lazy.

Infatuated *adj.* Possessed by an unreasoning love or attraction.

Infuse *v.* To inject; add to.

Inscrutable *adj.* Hard to interpret or understand; mysterious.

Instigate *v.* Stir up; provoke.

Intangible *adj.* Difficult to perceive, vague.

Interminable *adj.* Being or seeming to be without end; endless.

Intrigue *v.* To stir up the interest or curiosity of; fascinate.

J

Jangle *v.* To produce a harsh, discordant sound, as two comparatively small, thin, or hollow pieces of metal hitting together.

Jovial *adj.* Endowed with or characterized by a hearty, joyous humor or a spirit of good-fellowship.

L

Lament *v.* To express grief or deep regret.
Lodge *v.* To add imaginative details to; ornament.

Languorous *adj.* Creating a dreamy, lazy mood.
Lurk *v.* To lie hidden, ready to ambush.

Legitimate *adj.* Justifiable.

M

Magnanimous *adj.* Generous and noble.
Mystic *adj.* Inspiring a sense of mystery and wonder.

Meander *v.* To follow a winding path.

Mortified *adj.* Ashamed.

N

Naive *adj.* Simple in a natural perhaps foolish way; unsophisticated.

Noncommittal *adj.* Not revealing one's opinion or purpose.

O

Obscuring *adj.* Hiding from view; concealing.

P

Peremptorily *adj.* In a commanding manner.
Ponderous *adj.* Heavy in a clumsy way; bulky.

Prosaic *adj.* Dull; common.

Pernicious *adj.* Deadly; harmful.
Preclude *v.* To make impossible, especially by taking action in advance; prevent.
Proverbial *adj.* Wildly spoken of; famous.

Plagiarized *adj.* Taken from someone else's writings.
Proliferate *v.* To multiply or spread rapidly.

Punitive *adj.* Punishing or having to do with punishment.

Q

Questing *adj.* Journeying over; exploring.

R

Rapt *adj.* Deeply delighted; enchanted.
Reiterate *v.* To repeat.

Reprehensible *adj.* Deserving of blame.

Recite *v.* To say out loud something memorized.
Relent *v.* To become less harsh, strict or stubborn.
Resigned ad*v.* Accepting some condition or action as inevitable.

Regaled *adj.* Entertained or amused.
Repose *v.* To bring to view, to showtolie dead or at rest.
Ruinous *adj.* Bringing ruin or downfall; disastrous.

S

Sacrilegious *adj.* Disrespectful toward a sacred person, place or thing.
Squander *v.* To spend or use wastefully.

Subtle *adj.* Difficult to detect, usually because of the clever means employed; not obvious.
Sustain *v.* To keep alive; support.

Skewed *adj.* Distorted or slanted in a particular direction; unbalanced.
Stifle *v.* To smother; hold back.

Subversive *adj.* Intended or serving to overthrow established authority.

Slacken *v.* To slow down.

Stoicism *v.* Indifference to pleasure or pain; not showing emotion.
Sullen *adj.* Showing irritation or unhappiness by a gloomy silence; moody.

T

Tangible *adj.* Capable of being touched or felt; having actual form and substance.
Transcend *v.* To pass beyond the limits of; be greater than.

Tentative *adj.* Uncertain; hesitant.

Transcendent *adj.* Far above or beyond the usual and ordinary; supreme.

Tolerant *v.* Having or showing understanding and respect for other's customs or beliefs.
Transparent *adj.* Capable of being seen through.

U

Uncanny *adj.* So remarkable as to seem supernatural.

Unchecked *adj.* Not restrained or controlled.

Ungainly *adj.* Lacking grace; clumsily.

V

Vanquished *adj.* Defeated or

Vile *adj.* Evil; disgusting.

Virtuoso *adj.* Characteristic of

conquered.

a person with masterly knowledge or skill.

W

Wane *v.* To decrease gradually.

Wary *adj.* Cautious; watchful.

Wiliest *adj.* Most crafty or sly; trickiest.

Z

Zealous *adj.* Intensely devoted and enthusiastic.